W9-ATK-257

Eager Street Academy #884
401 East Eager Street
Baltimore, MD 21202

PINTEREST®:

How Ben Silbermann & Evan Sharp Changed the Way We Share What We Love

WIZARDS OF TECHNOLOGY

WIZARDS OF TECHNOLOGY

PINTEREST®:

How Ben Silbermann & Evan Sharp Changed the Way We Share What We Love

ROSA WATERS

Mason Crest

Mason Crest
450 Parkway Drive, Suite D
Broomall, PA 19008
www.masoncrest.com

Printed and bound in the USA.

First printing
9 8 7 6 5 4 3 2

Series ISBN: 978-1-4222-3178-4
ISBN: 978-1-4222-3185-2
ebook ISBN: 978-1-4222-8721-7

Library of Congress Cataloging-in-Publication Data

Waters, Rosa, 1957-
  Pinterest(tm) : how Ben Silbermann & Evan Sharp changed the way we share what we love / Rosa Waters.
    pages cm. — (Wizards of technology)
  ISBN 978-1-4222-3185-2 (hardback) — ISBN 978-1-4222-3178-4 (series) — ISBN 978-1-4222-8721-7 (ebook) 1. Pinterest—Juvenile literature. 2. Online social networks—Juvenile literature. 3. Silbermann, Ben—Juvenile literature. 4. Sharp, Evan—Juvenile literature. I. Title. II. Title: Pinterest trademark. III. Title: Pinterest.
  HM743.P56W38 2014
  006.7092'2—dc23
  [B]
                                        2014012230

CONTENTS

KEY ICONS TO LOOK FOR:

 Text-Dependent Questions: These questions send the reader back to the text for more careful attention to the evidence presented there.

 Words to Understand: These words with their easy-to-understand definitions will increase the reader's understanding of the text, while building vocabulary skills.

 Series Glossary of Key Terms: This back-of-the book glossary contains terminology used throughout this series. Words found here increase the reader's ability to read and comprehend higher-level books and articles in this field.

 Research Projects: Readers are pointed toward areas of further inquiry connected to each chapter. Suggestions are provided for projects that encourage deeper research and analysis.

 Sidebars: This boxed material within the main text allows readers to build knowledge, gain insights, explore possibilities, and broaden their perspectives by weaving together additional information to provide realistic and holistic perspectives.

Words to Understand

technology: Anything that humans invent to make something easier or achieve something new.

résumé: A record of a job applicant's past jobs and qualifications.

IT: Information technology—using computers to store and move information.

CHAPTER ONE

Beginnings

In just three short years, a small project with barely 5,000 users became one of the most popular websites on the Internet. The man behind this website had absolutely no background in business or technology before getting started. He did, however, have a very strong drive to succeed.

Ben Silbermann began developing Pinterest in 2009 with the help of Evan Sharp and Paul Sciarra. Together, they became the three co-founders of the website. It took just a few months for the first version of Pinterest to be built. The idea for Pinterest came to Ben shortly after he started his own company, Cold Brew Labs. He wanted to build something unique that the whole world could find useful.

Most of the social networking sites available at the time were all

Growing up, Ben looked up to technology and business pioneers like Steve Jobs.

about live updates. Users could post their likes and dislikes, but that was never the focus of other social networking websites. Ben wanted to create an outlet for creative people—and he did just that with Pinterest. Using his new website, users could share and collect images of everything that inspired them. Ben couldn't have predicted just how successful his small project would become!

BEN'S CHILDHOOD

When Ben was born, it seemed his path had already been chosen for him: he was going to be a doctor. "Both of my parents were doctors, and both of my sisters were doctors," he explained during a speech. Even his dad's parents were doctors! "I always assumed that I was going to be a doctor as well. I never even thought twice about it." Ben's parents, Jane and Neil, were both ophthalmologists, or eye doctors. They worked together at a family practice in Des Moines, Iowa.

Ben had many interests outside of medicine, though, such as **technology**, business, and collecting things. When the Internet began to boom in the 1990s, Ben was still in high school. He was soon hooked on the new information source.

He used the Internet to look up George Eastman, Walt Disney, and Steve Jobs because they were all successful entrepreneurs, people who had started their own businesses. Ben never thought he would start a business on his own, but he admired these men. "I always thought I didn't share anything in common with these people," he explained. "I looked up to them the same way I looked up to Michael Jordan."

According to Ben, he had a clear goal for his life before he even graduated from high school. "I was going to study really hard, and get into college, and then get into med school, and then become a doctor," he said.

Sometimes life surprises us!

When Ben first came to Yale University, he was on the path to be a doctor. But soon, he'd change his plans and move toward technology.

Make Connections

When Ben was a kid, he loved collecting things. Two of his favorite items to collect were insects and stamps. "Collecting tells a lot about who you are," he explained. Before the invention of Pinterest, Ben noticed, he said, that "there wasn't a place to share that side of who you are." Pinterest users can use the website to "pin" their interests on a pinboard, a little like a stamp or insect collection.

COLLEGE

After graduating from Roosevelt High School, Ben moved to the East Coast to study medicine at Yale University. At first, Ben was looking forward to being a doctor. He went above and beyond what was expected of him at school and developed a reputation as a dedicated student. "I took organic chemistry, and I worked in a lab every summer," he said. About two years into his degree, though, he started to really think about what his future would be like.

Becoming a doctor is tough work. People who want to become doctors need to earn an undergraduate degree and a graduate degree. Many future doctors need to spend more than ten years earning their degrees, and paying for all that education is very expensive. Students of medicine must also pass a lot of tests to ensure they are ready to work on living patients.

Ben's goals and hopes for the future changed drastically in his junior year of college. One morning, he woke up and thought, "I don't think I want to be a doctor." According to him, "It was the first time I'd ever really thought about it." Ben was two years into a medicine degree—and he didn't want to spend another moment earning a degree he just wasn't

Ben worked in Washington, D.C., after leaving school before moving to California.

interested in anymore. "My advice to anyone is that if there is ever a profession where you should really, really know that you want to do it, it's definitely medicine," he said.

Changing paths was not easy for Ben. Medicine was all he had ever really studied, so he felt lost in other subjects. Still, he hoped to one day achieve his new dream of becoming a successful businessman. He asked his friends for business advice and was told he should prepare a **résumé** and start going on job interviews.

Colleges and universities sometimes host job fairs where students can interview for companies that visit the school. Ben went to the fair, résumé in hand, and began talking to different companies. He had not done well in his finance classes, so he didn't think any job having to do with money would be a good fit for him. Ben looked into consulting and decided that was what he wanted to do.

Ben admits, "I had no idea what consulting was. I'd never met a consultant, so I didn't know what I was signing up for," but he was offered a job for a company in Washington, D.C., and he decided to take it. He graduated from Yale in 2003 with a degree in political science, and then he moved to D.C.

NEW VISIONS

His work responsibilities varied from day to day. "I had happened to be staffed in the **IT** group because that's where there were openings," he explained. Sometimes, he wrote out spreadsheets on the computer. Other days, he traveled all over the country.

During his free time at the office, Ben found himself remembering his boyhood passion for technology. He began reading about new companies that were just starting to gain popularity on the Internet. Some of his favorite websites to visit were weblogs, or blogs, where authors spoke about the next new inventions. Some of the first websites he learned about through a blog called TechCrunch were Digg and Yelp, both of which became successful soon after they were discovered.

Suddenly, Ben felt like he needed to move on. "I remember having this feeling that this was the story of my time and I was totally in the wrong place doing the wrong thing," he explained. Ben wanted to invent something new or develop a useful website, just like all of those other young entrepreneurs had done. He knew Washington, D.C., was not the right place to do it. He would need to move somewhere else to pursue his dreams.

Ben began researching his options. One night, he watched a movie with his girlfriend about Silicon Valley. The movie, titled *Pirates of Silicon*

Working at Google, Ben learned many things that would help him create and run Pinterest.

Valley, starred an actor who played Steve Jobs and an actor who played Bill Gates. The movie showcased how both these young men went on to own very successful technological businesses. They worked in an area of California that became known as Silicon Valley because of how many tech companies are stationed there.

The entrepreneurs in the movie inspired Ben, and he learned something very important: California was the place to be if he wanted to start a career in invention. Soon after watching the movie, he quit his job in Washington, D.C., and moved to the West Coast. His girlfriend, Divya, went with him to California.

Ben did not have a job lined up when he arrived in California, but he immediately fell in love with the atmosphere. Many of the people living in Silicon Valley were interested in invention too. "Being surrounded by so many people who were so passionate about it was a really big deal," he explained. Their passion helped push Ben to pursue his own dreams.

WORKING FOR GOOGLE

Google was growing steadily by the time Ben arrived in California. Ben dreamed of working for the company, which was best known for its creative inventions and popular search engine. "I thought Google was the coolest place," he said. "People there were so smart and they were all

Make Connections

Silicon Valley is located on the West Coast of the United States, in northern California. It was originally named after the many silicon-chip innovators and manufacturers that were based in the area. Many new companies hoping to find success in the world of technology get their start in Silicon Valley.

Text-Dependent Questions

1. How long ago did the co-founders of Pinterest begin working on the website?
2. Why did Ben always assume he would be a doctor when he grew up?
3. Which of Ben's childhood interests later influenced the invention of Pinterest?
4. Why did Ben decide to leave Washington, D.C., and move to Silicon Valley?
5. Explain why working at Google was both inspiring and frustrating for Ben.

doing these really interesting things." Ben wanted to do interesting things too.

Unfortunately, it would be hard for Ben to land a job at Google because he didn't have a computer science or engineering background. All he had was a political science degree and some experience at a consulting job in Washington, D.C. Even though the odds were against him, though, Ben wasn't ready to give up on his dream just yet. He decided to go on a job interview anyway, hoping there would be a fit for him in the large company.

During Ben's interview, the interviewer asked Ben why he wanted to work at Google. He replied simply, "I love the Internet." After the interview, he was offered the job, and began working in customer support. Ben believes one of the reasons he was given the job over other applicants is because of how enthusiastic he was. It was clear that he wanted to work at Google more than anyone else, so he was given the job!

Ben's time at Google was spent on many tasks, but the projects he worked most on were product design recommendations. He listened to feedback from people who used Google products, and then he made

Research Project

During his time in Washington, D.C., Ben realized that he needed to move to Silicon Valley to pursue his dream. Using the Internet, research the history of Silicon Valley. List at least five successful companies that got started there. Explain why so many technological companies are stationed in the Bay area of San Francisco.

suggestions to the design team so they could make those products even better. Unfortunately, Ben was never allowed to work on these products directly because he didn't have the background to do it. This frustrated Ben. He just wanted to invent something new!

Despite his frustration, Ben loved working at Google. "I think that Google was and still is a really special place," he said. "At Google I think the lesson that I learned is that they dream really big." The technology of an expanding Internet was being put to use in almost every product Google created. "You can connect with people that might be really far away, and that was really exciting," he said.

This excitement never left Ben. It gave him the energy and inspiration to start something of his own.

Words to Understand

investors: People who put money into a business, hoping that the business will make the money back.

stock market: The marketplace where shares of companies are bought and sold.

persistent: Trying hard, even when things aren't going well.

potential: Able to be something more in the future.

engineering: The study or job of designing or improving technologies.

chronological: In order of time.

real time: Happening as they happen in real life.

urgency: Importance requiring fast action.

CHAPTER TWO

Starting Small

Ben enjoyed being on the forefront of technology, but merely making suggestions at Google was not enough for him. He wanted to actually build something himself. He often expressed his concerns to his girlfriend, Divya, who one day told him, "You should stop talking about it and go do it."

Ben listened to Divya's advice. He now credits her with giving him the push he needed to start his own company. "I left my job, which was the best job I ever had, to go do it," he said. Ben took a big risk when he quit his job, but he knew he needed to leave Google to pursue his dreams. Unfortunately, his timing couldn't have been worse.

A few weeks after Ben quit his job at Google, the economy started taking a turn for the worse. **Investors** lost a lot of money in the **stock market**. Some of Ben's friends at Google had agreed to leave their jobs

Ben's first work in building a business in the technology world focused on creating smartphone apps.

to come join him if his new company took off, but now they did not want to leave. Joining Ben at a startup company was far too risky for them now.

Funding his new company was also proving to be more difficult than he had imagined. "It was pretty much impossible to raise money," he explained. "The funding environment was really hard because traditionally the people that invest money are pretty wealthy themselves and they just lost all this money in the stock market."

No one wanted to invest in Ben's new ideas, but he was determined to make it work anyway. He named his new company Cold Brew Labs and went to work.

Ben did have a piece of good luck, though. "I worked on a bunch of ideas alone, and I eventually hooked up with a friend of mine from college, but he was from New York." That friend was Paul Sciarra, who would later be known as one of the three founders of Pinterest. Paul was still living in Silicon Valley, so communicating with him needed to be done through e-mails and phone conversations.

TOTE

One of the first projects Ben and Paul worked on was Tote. It was an application, or app, designed for the iPhone. Tote's aim was to allow users to look up any product they wanted using a phone. At the time, nothing like it existed, so Ben hoped he would release the first app of its kind. It would be a great application when released—but actually finishing it was proving to be difficult.

Ben encountered two problems while working on Tote. First, he needed to index every item he could get his hands on. Ben went to retail stores in order to catalogue each item in the store. At times, it felt like he had bitten off more than he could chew. There were thousands of items in each store, and he was doing all the hard work alone while Paul was in New York.

The second problem Ben faced was actually getting his creation

Ben had trouble with the time it took to get Tote approved for sale on Apple's App Store.

released to the public. All iPhone applications needed to be reviewed by Apple before they were made available in the application store. "Apps had just been released so the approval process was taking months and months and months," Ben said. All Ben and Paul could do was wait for the day customers could actually start using Tote.

Meanwhile, the money Ben had saved from working with Google was quickly dwindling. He needed to find money elsewhere, so he turned to investors. One lesson Ben learned early on was that he needed to be **persistent** if he wanted to get anywhere. "I think I can safely say that I talked to every single investor in Silicon Valley," he recalled of his early days with Cold Brew Labs.

Unfortunately, investors were unwilling to put money into a company that hadn't really accomplished anything yet. Still, Ben pushed on. He didn't want to give up on his dreams, and he didn't want Paul to give up either. "My friend Paul had made the jump as well, and I didn't want to let him down," he said.

One of the hardest lessons a new business owner must learn is when to give up on an idea that just isn't going to work out. After a few months of hard work, it was clear that Tote was not going to be as successful as Ben and Paul hoped it would be. Though it was hard to do, Ben and Paul abandoned Tote in order to focus their efforts on a new project. Hopefully, the new project would be more successful than Tote had been!

STARTING PINTEREST

Ben spent weeks trying to find investors willing to put money into his company, but not a single person wanted to invest. Then, finally, one company was willing to give him a chance. Once one investor had signed on, it was easier to gain other supporters. Ben seized the opportunity to call up companies that had previously denied him to ask them to invest again.

Ben had a few strategies to lure in potential investors. Two of his favorite phrases were, "You're going to miss out" and, "This is a hot deal."

Ben has worked hard to follow his dreams of building his own company. He encourages other young people to do the same and believe in their own passions.

Surprisingly, it worked. By telling **potential** investors that they only had a limited time to invest, they were more likely to give him money upfront.

Once Ben had enough money to continue working, it was time to pick a new project to work on. Although Ben always thought Tote was a good idea, he never truly felt passionate about it. With his new project, Ben said he would, "try to build something I had always wanted to build." He thought back to his love of collecting as a child and imagined what

Make Connections: Bet on Yourself

When Ben was growing up, his parents encouraged him to follow his dreams, even if it meant taking risks in the process. According to Ben, one of the most important lessons his parents taught him was: "If you don't bet on yourself, nobody else will."

collections would look like on the Internet. No one had ever built a website showcasing collections before. His idea could be the first.

At about the same time, Ben met Evan Sharp, who would later become known as the third founder of Pinterest. Evan was a talented architect working in New York. He was very interested in Ben's ideas for the future of Pinterest. He communicated with Ben using e-mails and telephone calls, just like Paul had done.

One day, Evan finally asked Ben, "Where do we start?" Building a website takes quite a bit of time and effort, and Ben did not have a computer science background. Fortunately, Evan was a very talented designer, and he took over the *engineering* aspect of the job. He propelled Pinterest forward by asking questions like, "What's the one thing that is most important?"

Ben and Evan's different interests and talents made Pinterest what it is today. Like Ben, Evan was a collector as a child. When Ben suggested a website based on virtual collections, Evan developed Ben's ideas into a useful website using his own background in design. Together, Ben, Evan, and Paul made a great team.

PINTEREST DESIGN

A website showcasing collections of all sorts could take many different forms. Evan suggested a grid layout to make the website easy to use.

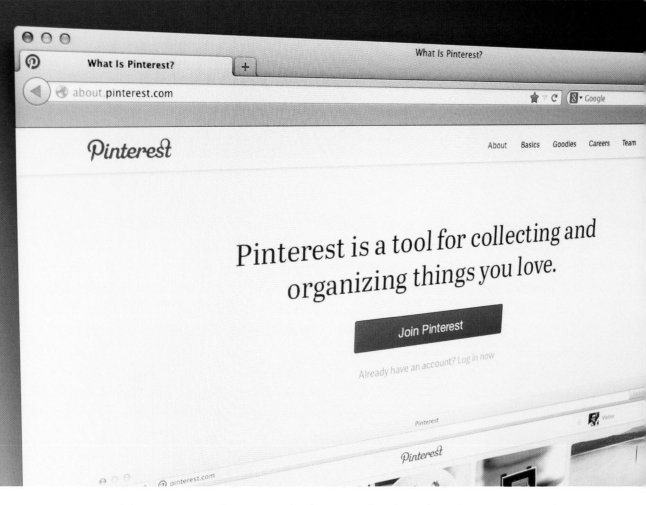

Pinterest didn't come together overnight, but Ben's hard work and previous mistakes would pay off soon.

Grids are made up of columns and rows. According to Evan, every detail of the first layout was carefully planned. The size of each box, as well as the location of the text in that box, was no accident. Even the colors used were thought through.

Make Connections

Evan Sharp studied history at the University of Chicago and then architecture at Columbia. Before Pinterest, he worked as an architect, but he also had experience as a product designer at Facebook.

Making a website was proving to be more difficult than they'd thought, though. Ben hired an additional engineer to help with the job, but it still took his team of four a total of three or four months to finish the first version of Pinterest.

The first people to receive access to the website were friends and family of the owners. Pinterest purposefully restricted how fast people could sign up. For a long time, users could only join through receiving an invitation from someone else.

By the time the website was done, Ben began to notice a trend that worried him. Many of the most popular websites on the Internet in 2010 were based on a *chronological* model. Users could post updates about their lives in *real time* using text, images, or video. Two examples of these websites were Facebook and Twitter. Pinterest, on the other hand, was not about real-time updates. Would people be willing to accept its differences?

Pinterest was first released to the public in March of 2010, but at first, it was not as popular as Ben had hoped. Users still needed to be invited to the website in order to join, and very few people were interested. They did not see the need for a website like Pinterest when other, more popular social media options were available. A few months after launch, the

Pinterest allows users to "pin" their favorite things to a digital corkboard, collecting the things they love and want to show others online.

Make Connections

The website Pinterest is a combination of the words "pin" and "interest." Users can pin anything they find interesting on a personalized user page known as a pinboard for anyone else to see. Other users can then click on these pinned items, and either pin it to their own pages or like it to show their support. Users can also give friends permission to pin items to their pages if those pages are being used for specific purposes.

website had grown to only 5,000 users. Many of the first users of Pinterest were from Ben's hometown of Des Moines, which Ben suggests may have been a result of his mother telling her patients about his website.

If Ben was ever going to turn Pinterest into a success, he needed to find an answer to the most important question of all: how could he get more users interested in the idea of virtual collections?

PIN IT FORWARD

In May of 2010, Ben was given the chance to show the world what Pinterest could do. A campaign known as "Pin It Forward" was started to introduce Pinterest to new users. Users who participated in "Pin It Forward" were invited to make a pinboard of their very own based on what "home meant to them."

The targeted users for Pin It Forward were bloggers, or people who wrote on weblogs and online journals about a wide variety of topics. Like pinboards, blogs are often focused on one specific subject, making bloggers the perfect target for Pinterest's growth. Many new users were creative with the project, creating pinboards that Ben's team couldn't have imagined.

Research Project

When Pinterest first began, it was made up of only three people working out of a small house. It quickly grew, and now the company has dozens of full-time employees in a large San Francisco office. Using the Internet, research how many employees Pinterest currently has. Is the company currently hiring? If so, what type of employees are they looking for? What jobs at Pinterest look interesting to you? Use the Internet or library to find out what kind of education and experience you would need for those jobs.

Throughout Pinterest's growth, Ben never lost sight of the end goal. He always envisioned Pinterest as "the place to plan the most important projects in your life," whether those projects involved clothing, travel, or cooking. Users who were flocking to Pinterest had found their own specific use for the website, and their feedback would only help the website get better.

By the end of 2010, Pinterest had 10,000 users and was finally showing potential. The company itself had still grown very little, though. It was based out of a small house in Silicon Valley. Ben's team would need to keep pushing if they wanted Pinterest to grow in popularity. One of the mottos of the growing company became, "Move Fast and Break Things." The motto was on a poster that hung in Pinterest's tiny office.

Consumer input was very important to Ben, so he e-mailed each one of those first 5,000 users of Pinterest, asking for their feedback and offering to communicate with them directly. He spoke with some users on the phone and met others in person. He then took their feedback to his own team so they could use it to improve the website.

All these changes needed to be made fast, which is why Ben stressed

Text-Dependent Questions

1. What caused Ben to quit Google and start his own company?
2. What challenges did Ben face while trying to develop Tote?
3. Why did Ben need the help of investors and how did he go about getting funding?
4. What role did Evan play in the startup of Pinterest?
5. What is Pin It Forward and how did it help Pinterest grow?

the importance of urgency to his team. "It's really important to keep people focused on what's important and what's not important," he says of his experience managing creative people. "Teaching a team to operate with that level of *urgency* without burning people out is just something that's really important."

Pin it

Words to Understand

diverse: Having a wide range of different people or things.
execute: Make something happen.
integrate: Mix different things together to make a single whole.
harassment: Aggressive pressure or intimidation.
evolves: Changes over time.
skeptical: Not easily convinced of something.

CHAPTER THREE

Growing Fast

The year 2011 started out well for Ben's team. They received a lot of money from investors who were finally seeing the value of what Pinterest could offer to the world. The company received millions of dollars of funding to help it expand. This money allowed Ben to hire more people, move to a larger office, and greatly improve his website.

Ben didn't just stumble upon millions of dollars of funding; he earned it through hard work and planning. "We would show them real users," he explained. By introducing investors to people who actually used Pinterest, he would be able to show the investors firsthand why people were interested in the product, and why it would continue to expand.

Pinterest's smartphone app has helped the company reach more people and kept old users coming back.

WHEN DREAMS COME TRUE

In just one short year, Pinterest grew from 10,000 users to millions of visits per week. *Time Magazine* took notice of Pinterest's popularity and named Pinterest as one of the "50 Best Websites of 2011" in August of that year. The site continued to grow, and by December it was considered one of the top-ten largest social networking websites, putting it on the same level as Facebook, Google+, and Youtube. Ben's dream was becoming a reality!

Even after Pinterest became a popular website that millions of people spent time on each day, Ben stressed the importance of life outside the Internet. According to him, the mission of Pinterest is "not to keep you online," but to "get you offline." "Pinterest," he said, "should inspire you to go out and do things you love."

Ben has always hoped that users of Pinterest who saw something interesting on the site would feel inspired to actually do that thing. For example, they might make a new meal after seeing a picture of a delicious recipe, or go on a trip after seeing pictures of a travel location.

MORE EXPANSION

In 2011, Ben decided again to release an application for the iPhone. This time, it was based on his growing website, Pinterest. He believed the new application would bring more users to the website, but he couldn't have imagined just how much the iPhone app would help his company grow.

The iPhone app was released in March, and it was so successful that a mobile version of the website was built for smartphone users who had iPhones. The grid layout of the Pinterest website turned out to be the perfect layout for a smartphone or tablet user. All of the pinned items were easy to click and view, even without the use of a mouse.

In August of 2012, Ben changed the website in another way when he opened it up to all users. People who wanted to join Pinterest no longer needed an invitation from a friend. They could simply go to the website

Pinterest has worked to keep up with new technology, like tablet computers and smartphones.

Make Connections

Many startup companies hope that one day larger, more powerful companies will buy them. The founders of these companies aim to make a profit off of the start of a very good idea. Unfortunately, very few larger companies choose to buy small companies while they are still growing. In Pinterest's early days, Ben tried to sell Pinterest for a profit, but not a single company offered him enough money for the startup idea. The founders of Pinterest continued to manage the company on their own, and it's a good thing they did! Today, Pinterest is estimated to be worth almost four billion dollars.

and sign up. That same month, a Pinterest application was introduced for the Android operating system, which is made by Google. An iPad tablet version was released as well.

EMPLOYEES

One of the ways Ben has kept Pinterest new and fresh is by hiring people who have previously worked for larger, more established companies. Ben came from Google, and so have some of his other employees. Evan Sharp had once worked with Facebook. Jon Jenkins, a head engineer hired in 2012, was originally from Amazon. While many employees come from other companies, some, though, have never worked anywhere else.

Ben believes that, "the best things in the world are made by groups of people," which is why he hires a *diverse* set of people to work for his company. What he looks for most in new employees is the passion and drive to work on a project they love. Ben is very grateful for his team. He has said, "I feel genuinely lucky to walk into the office and work with people that are better than me at pretty much everything I do." While

Ben has worked hard to become a success in the competitive world of online business, and all at a very early age.

Ben may come up with great ideas, he credits his team with finding ways to *execute* those ideas.

THE WEBSITE

Plenty of features have been added to Pinterest since it was first launched in 2010. The grid design, a staple of the site, has been greatly improved over the years, allowing users to interact with each other more directly. Users who find a pinboard they like can now follow it. Any pinboards that users follow will show up in Pinterest's "pin feed," a main page for the website.

One of the first challenges Ben met when creating Pinterest was getting new people interested. People who had used websites like Facebook and Twitter saw no reason for Pinterest, so Ben did his best to *integrate* Pinterest with other websites. Users who pin something to Pinterest now have the option of posting a notification on their Facebook and Twitter pages about it. This encourages even more people to visit Pinterest, even those who wouldn't have otherwise thought of going to the website.

As Pinterest grew in popularity, businesses began finding reasons to use the website too. New products and deals could be posted on the company's pinboard, with the option to go to the company's website to actually buy something. Even users who didn't plan to buy the product might repin something of interest to notify their followers of the great deal.

At first, businesses needed to create a normal user account, but in September of 2012, Pinterest introduced business accounts. Any company that already had an account was given the option to convert that account to a business account, or start over with a completely new account. The addition of business accounts made it even easier for companies to use Pinterest for their needs.

Pinterest users are as diverse as their interests. However, some interesting trends can be seen. One study showed that as many as 80 percent

Pinterest works hard to protect the artists who share their work on the website, keeping their work from being copied by others illegally.

Make Connections: Co-Founders

One of Pinterest's co-founders, Paul Sciarra, left the company in 2012. Ben Silbermann and Evan Sharp remained at the company, with Ben becoming the CEO and Evan taking on the role of lead designer.

of people who use Pinterest are women. It is hard to say why the website has become so popular with women in particular, but it may be because their interests are more available on Pinterest at the current time. Some of the most popular pinboards in 2012 were about food, crafts, clothes, and travel. As Pinterest grows, so will the pinboards, and perhaps men will be more interested in future collections featured on the website.

PROTECTING USERS AND ARTISTS

Social networking websites allow users from all over the world to communicate with each other. Web developers hope that these websites will be used in a positive way, but that isn't always the case. Some people may be unkind toward others, or downright rude. Pinterest introduced a new feature in October of 2012 that would allow users to block others. There is also an option to report someone for *harassment*.

Users aren't the only people Pinterest cares about protecting. Pinterest encourages creative people to share their ideas with the world, which means other users might copy artists' work without their consent. Pinterest introduced plenty of countermeasures as a result.

One interesting way Pinterest combats copyright infringement is by allowing other webpages to include a code in their images. This code

Pinterest has succeeded by being different from many other social networking websites.

Make Connections: Visual Design

Many social media websites encourage users to write text posts. Images and video may also be posted, but the focus is primarily about what someone writes. Pinterest is completely different; the focus of the website is completely visual. Large images and links make up the majority of a pinboard. Images may be posted with text, but that text is always much smaller than the image.

prevents that image from being pinned anywhere on Pinterest. Many large websites have used this code, including Flickr, an image-hosting website.

But that didn't fix every problem. Some images that were allowed to be pinned were not showing their origin, and thus not giving credit where it was due. Pinterest added the option for credit to automatically be given to images and videos that came from certain websites. Some of these websites were Youtube, Vimeo, Flickr, and Behance.

Like Pinterest, the Internet *evolves* with each passing day. The needs of the website and its users will change over time, which is why Ben and his team are committed to keeping the website safe and fun for everyone. The community is meant to be friendly, not dangerous, and it should promote creativity, not steal it.

BEING DIFFERENT

When Pinterest was first launched, users noticed that it was unlike any of the other popular social media sites. It didn't update in real time, there was no live feed, and it didn't use text to connect users to one another. Instead, it used pictures and images to tell a user's story. In many ways,

Text-Dependent Questions

1. What honor did *Time Magazine* give to Pinterest in August of 2011?
2. List at least three large companies Pinterest employees have previously worked at. Why does Ben hire a diverse group of people?
3. How have businesses used Pinterest to their advantage?
4. Name two of the ways Pinterest has protected users and artists on the website.
5. What milestone did Pinterest reach in March of 2012, and why was it important?

Pinterest was the polar opposite of Facebook and Twitter, the two most popular social networks at the time.

The first people to look at Pinterest were *skeptical* about where it would go because of how different it was from what they were used to. The website clearly didn't follow the model that had been successful over the past few years, so some users were finding it difficult to adjust to Pinterest. Fortunately, Ben and Evan were able to help the world see the benefits of using Pinterest.

In March 2012, Pinterest reached a new milestone when it became the third largest social networking website on the Internet, proving that it didn't have to follow the same model as other social networking websites to become popular. "One of the most satisfying realizations is that there are a lot of different ways to succeed," Ben said. The only two websites ahead of Pinterest now were Facebook and Twitter (although that could always change).

Even though Pinterest proved that not all social networking websites needed to follow the same model, it was not rigid in its design. It changed

Research Project

Pinterest has changed a lot since it was first released in 2010. Using the Internet, research some of the recent features added to Pinterest. Why were these features implemented, and how will they change the way people use Pinterest in the future?

and developed as Ben's team learned how users were using the website. Pinterest has become a network, a community, like other social networking websites. It's not just about collecting anymore.

"It's not what we thought the site was going to do when we first launched it, but it's what it's come to be," Ben said.

Ben describes his team as a group of people who "want to build something bigger than themselves." Pinterest has become a whole new culture, and the original creators are not entirely in control of how that culture changes. This doesn't bother Ben, though, who has said that, "Sometimes, the product finds its purpose, and sometimes it goes the other way around. Either way is okay, as long as you get to something that people really love."

Words to Understand

critics: People who express negative opinions of something.
monetize: Start making money from a website or service.
relevant: Mattering to the current circumstances.
intrusive: Unwelcome or annoying.
cater: Address a certain person's or group's needs.

CHAPTER FOUR

The Future
of Pinterest

Pinterest has made its mark as one of the fastest-expanding websites in the history of the Internet. In just a few short years, it went from a simple idea three people worked on to having millions of users. At the start of 2014, it reported having a total of twenty-five billion individual pins. The website, which is now on the same popularity level as Facebook and Twitter, shows no signs of slowing down.

Pinterest began buying other websites in 2013, starting with Livestar in March. Livestar was a mobile application that could be used to give and read recommendations to friends, family, and *critics*. These recommendations could be for anything from restaurants to movies and music.

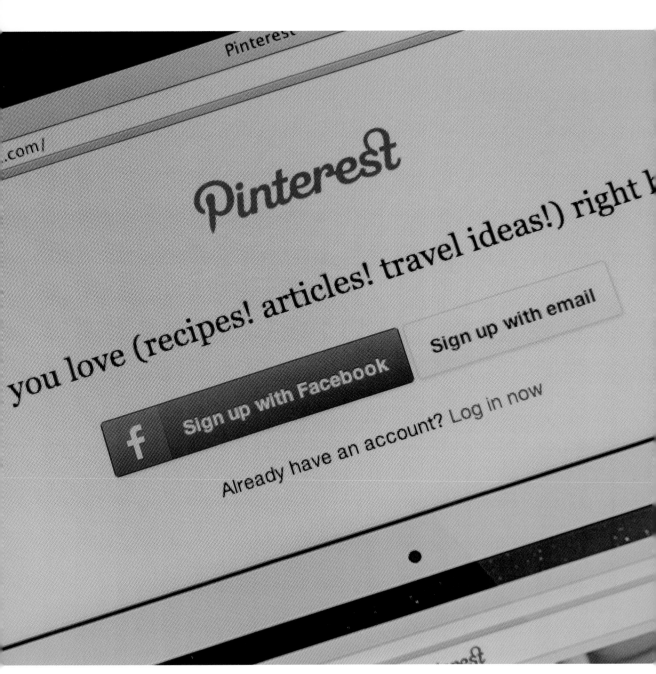

Today, Pinterest has become one of the most popular social networking websites on the Internet.

Make Connections: Ben's Advice to Young People

Many young entrepreneurs one day would love to follow in Ben's footsteps. As a co-founder of Pinterest, Ben has been asked to give speeches to people who want to learn something from his story. At the end of one of these speeches, he offered two pieces of advice. First, "Build something you believe in." Building a company from the ground up can take many years, so it is important that you stay interested and passionate about what you do. His other piece of advice is, "Don't give up." Ben wouldn't have gotten anywhere if he gave up on Pinterest during its first few months.

Another company Pinterest bought was Hackermeter. Like Pinterest, Hackermeter's greatest use was to bring people together around whatever interested them. In Hackermeter's case, it brought developers and employers together to collaborate on projects. People with great ideas like Pinterest would have an easier time getting them off the ground using the tools Hackermeter had to offer.

When Hackermeter was bought in October, that company's co-founders were brought into Pinterest as well. They will work as engineers and help make Pinterest even better than it once was. Like Pinterest, Hackermeter sports a simple, visually appealing website that is easy to use and navigate.

MAKING MONEY

Keeping a large website like Pinterest running is not cheap. The content is provided to users for free, so Pinterest has to come up with a way to make money somehow. For a very long time, Pinterest was not making any sort of profit. Its goal was to grow as big as possible, even as millions

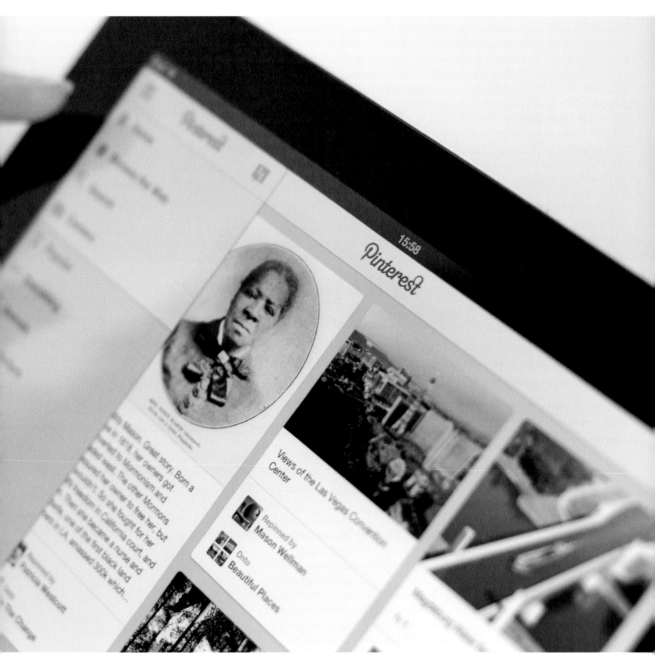

Millions of people around the world are sharing their favorite things on Pinterest each day, whether on tablets, smartphones, or home computers.

While many businesses have looked to advertising or subscriptions to make money online, Pinterest is taking its time to find the best way to make money.

of dollars were invested in a company that investors hoped would one day be profitable.

Jon Jenkins, the head engineer at Pinterest, explained during an interview why the company wasn't looking to make money yet: "We're extremely fortunate to be well funded right now. It gives us time to do this correctly. We don't feel the pressure to *monetize* unnaturally." In other

Pinterest has become a hugely successful Internet business. Few companies have had as much impact online as Pinterest.

Make Connections

Pinterest was originally created to help people connect online, but now it has become much more than that. Many Pinterest users choose to bring that community to the physical world by meeting people they have only known on the Internet. Pinterest even has a section of their website dedicated to these meetups, which are designed to help people with similar interests connect with one another on a real, personal level.

words, Pinterest did not want to make money in a way that would go against the spirit of Pinterest.

Many social networking websites turn to ads or sponsored links to make money, but Pinterest has chosen to follow a slightly different path. In 2013, Ben spoke about a future business model for Pinterest. According to him, "There is a direct link between the things you pin and the things you eventually spend money on." If Pinterest can find a way to make money off what people pin, then everyone will be happy.

One of the ways Pinterest might make money in the future is by introducing promoted pins. Companies would be able to pay Pinterest a certain amount of money to show these pins above other pins on popular pinboards. Because these pins would be *relevant* to the pinboards they are posted on, it wouldn't be *intrusive*, unlike the advertisements that are displayed on other social networking websites.

As time goes on, Pinterest will likely buy more small companies. The ideas brought to Pinterest by these companies could help Pinterest expand, or even find new ways to bring money to the company. In 2013,

Pinterest Explained: Q&A with

Young people looking to make their way in the world of online business now look to Ben as an inspiration the way he looked to his heroes like Steve Jobs and Bill Gates.

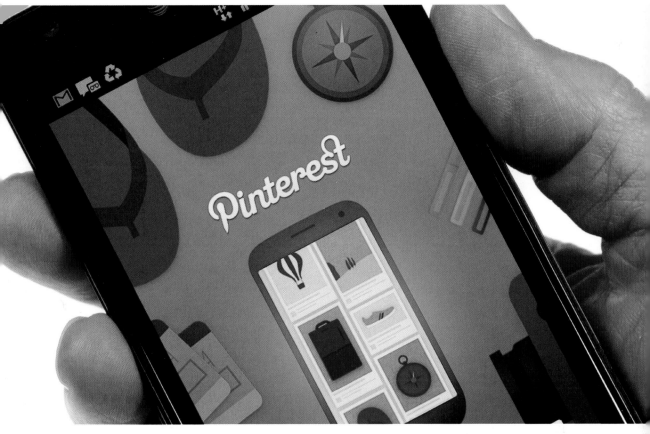

While Pinterest has millions of users and billions of dollars from investors, Ben still has to work hard to keep the company successful.

Pinterest was worth about $3.8 billion thanks to the investments of people who believed in Pinterest from the start.

WHAT COMES NEXT?

How people use Pinterest has changed a lot since the website was first released to the public. Pinterest's motto has always been, "Pinterest is a tool for collecting and organizing things you love." What people love can be pretty diverse, so Pinterest does its best to **cater** to everyone's needs.

For someone who is new to Pinterest, it can be hard to know where to get started. That's why Pinterest offers a few examples of how actual people are using Pinterest. Users can make a pinboard to show what clothes they want to buy, the locations where they want to travel, the events they want to plan, and what collections they have started. No project is too big or too small for a pinboard.

One of the concerns of people who use Pinterest is that pinboards are not at all private. Anyone with a link to a pinboard can use it, and there is no way to block someone from visiting your own personal page. This might be fine if you make a pinboard about your favorite movies, but not if you are using it to plan a special event in your life. For this reason, don't post anything too personal on Pinterest!

During an interview, one user asked Ben if Pinterest ever has plans to add privacy settings. He said it was something they are considering, but that it will take some time. He didn't want to add too many privacy options, or users might get confused. He'd rather stick with a select few that are easy to understand and add to the site.

Ben is a businessman who stands by his product and uses it regularly

Research Project

Pinterest has started to expand beyond its own borders by buying other startup companies. Using the Internet, research Pinterest's latest purchases. Which companies has Pinterest bought in the last year, and how might buying these companies help Pinterest in the future?

himself. When Divya and Ben were engaged to be married, they made a pinboard to help them plan their future wedding. Now that they have a son named Max, Ben uses Pinterest to learn about parenthood. Ben has specific interests that make him want to use Pinterest.

Thousands of users have their own interests too—and Pinterest has a place for them all. And it's all possible because of a man who didn't want to be a doctor!

FIND OUT MORE

In Books

Carr, Kelby. *Pinterest for Dummies*. Hoboken, N.J.: John Wiley & Sons, 2012.

Hayden, Beth. *Pinfluence: The Complete Guide to Marketing Your Business with Pinterest*. Hoboken, N.J.: John Wiley & Sons, 2012.

Rosenberg, Scott. *Say Everything: How Blogging Began, What It's Becoming, and Why It Matters*. New York: Three Rivers, 2009.

Selfridge, Benjamin, and Peter Selfridge. *A Kid's Guide to Creating Web Pages for Home and School*. Chicago: Zephyr, 2004.

Topper, Hilary. *Everything You Ever Wanted to Know about Social Media, but Were Afraid to Ask*. Bloomington, Ind.: Iuniverse, 2009.

On the Internet

Ben Silbermann
www.thextraordinary.org/ben-silbermann

Business Inside: "Meet Ben Silbermann, The Brilliant Young Co-Founder of Pinterest"
www.businessinsider.com/pinterest-2012-3

Fortune: "Is Pinterest the Next Facebook?"
tech.fortune.cnn.com/2012/03/22/pinterest-silbermann-photo-sharing

Pinterest
www.pinterest.com

USA Today: "Pinterest Stands Out In Crowded Social Media Field"
usatoday30.usatoday.com/tech/news/story/2011-10-28/
pinterest-Ben-Silbermann/50979542/1

SERIES GLOSSARY
OF KEY TERMS

application: A program that runs on a computer or smartphone. People often call these "apps."

bug: A problem with how a program runs.

byte: A unit of information stored on a computer. One byte is equal to eight digits of binary code—that's eight 1s or 0s.

cloud: Data and apps that are stored on the Internet instead of on your own computer or smartphone are said to be "in the cloud."

data: Information stored on a computer.

debug: Find the problems with an app or program and fix them.

device: Your computer, smartphone, or other piece of technology. Devices can often access the Internet and run apps.

digital: Having to do with computers or stored on a computer.

hardware: The physical part of a computer. The hardware is made up of the parts you can see and touch.

memory: Somewhere that a computer stores information that it is using.

media: Short for multimedia, it's the entertainment or information that can be stored on a computer. Examples of media include music, videos, and e-books.

network: More than one computer or device connected together so information can be shared between them.

pixel: A dot of light or color on a digital display. A computer monitor or phone screen has lots of pixels that work together to create an image.

program: A collection of computer code that does a job.

software: Programs that run on a computer.

technology: Something that people invent to make a job easier or do something new.

INDEX

ABOUT THE AUTHOR

Aurelia Jackson is a writer living and working in New York City. She has a passion for writing and a love of education, both of which she brings to all the work she does.

PICTURE CREDITS

Dreamstime.com:
6: GilbertC
8: Featureflash
12: Sjohnwilkin
14: Sebastian Czapnik
20: Chimeandsense
22: Jakub Jirsák
26: Dolphfyn
28: Ginasanders
32: Koolander
34: Marcel De Grijs
36: Marcel De Grijs
40: Yap Kee Chan

42: GilbertC
46: Gary Arbach
48: GilbertC
50: Viorel Dudau
51: Pressureua
52: Pressureua
55: Gary Arbach

Flickr.com:
24: Anya
54: Anya

38: Fast Company Magazine